THE ANIMAL FILES

WE NEED
BEES

by Lisa Bullard

FOCUS READERS

WWW.FOCUSREADERS.COM

Focus Readers is distributed by North Star Editions:
sales@northstareditions.com | 888-417-0195

Produced for Focus Readers by Red Line Editorial.

Content Consultant: Thomas D. Seeley, Horace White Professor in Biology, Cornell University

Photographs ©: SumikoPhoto/iStockphoto, cover, 1; Pee Tongsadayu/iStockphoto, 4–5; Hans Geel/Shutterstock Images, 7 (burger); Andrey_Kuzmin/Shutterstock Images, 7 (milk); Volosina/Shutterstock Images, 7 (yogurt with berries); Nataly Studio/Shutterstock Images, 7 (apple); Winai Pantho/Shutterstock Images, 9; Igor Marusichenko/Shutterstock Images, 10–11; Sushitsky Sergey/Shutterstock Images, 13; Red Line Editorial, 14; nata-lunata/Shutterstock Images, 17; TopPhoto/AP Images, 18–19; Fotokostic/Shutterstock Images, 20; Photografiero/Shutterstock Images, 22; kosolovskyy/Shutterstock Images, 24–25; Zakhar Mar/Shutterstock Images, 27; I. Rottlaender/Shutterstock Images, 28

Library of Congress Cataloging-in-Publication Data
Names: Bullard, Lisa, author.
Title: We need bees / by Lisa Bullard.
Description: Lake Elmo, MN : Focus Readers, [2019] | Series: The animal files
  | Audience: Grade 4 to 6. | Includes index.
Identifiers: LCCN 2018027808 (print) | LCCN 2018027996 (ebook) | ISBN
  9781641854849 (PDF) | ISBN 9781641854269 (e-book) | ISBN 9781641853101
  (hardcover : alk. paper) | ISBN 9781641853682 (paperback : alk. paper)
Subjects: LCSH: Bees--Ecology--Juvenile literature. |
  Bees--Conservation--Juvenile literature.
Classification: LCC QL565.2 (ebook) | LCC QL565.2 .B85 2019 (print) | DDC
  595.79/9--dc23
LC record available at https://lccn.loc.gov/2018027808

Printed in the United States of America
Mankato, MN
October, 2018

ABOUT THE AUTHOR

Lisa Bullard is the author of more than 90 books for children, including the mystery novel *Turn Left at the Cow*. She also teaches writing classes for adults and children. Lisa grew up in Minnesota and now lives just north of Minneapolis.

TABLE OF CONTENTS

CHAPTER 1

THE SUPER POLLINATOR

A bee lands on a blooming sunflower. It is collecting the flower's **pollen**. The powdery pollen clings to the bee's body. Then the bee flies to another sunflower. Some pollen from the first flower falls onto the second flower. The bee collects more pollen. It moves on again, spreading pollen from plant to plant.

Sunflowers are an excellent source of pollen for bees.

Approximately 20,000 **species** of bees exist on Earth. All bee species eat **nectar** from flowering plants. Most bees also gather pollen for food. But the bees are not only helping themselves. Many foods that humans eat come from flowering plants. Some examples are apples, almonds, and cucumbers. The plants that these foods come from need to be pollinated. Pollination happens when pollen from one plant is moved to another plant. Trading pollen allows the plants to grow seeds and fruit.

Bees help produce other foods as well. For example, bees pollinate a plant called alfalfa. Beef cattle and dairy cows eat alfalfa. These animals provide humans with meat and dairy products. Without bees, humans would have fewer food choices. They might not get the nutrients they need.

BEES BRING THE FOOD

Bee pollination helped produce the following foods:

yogurt

ketchup

pickles

beef

blueberries

milk

apples

Bees help create nonfood products, too. For example, some bees pollinate cotton plants. Humans then make the cotton into clothing. Some bee-pollinated plants are also used to make medicines.

Bees are not the only pollinators. Insects such as flies and butterflies also spread pollen. Birds and bats are pollinators, too. Some pollination occurs without animals. For example, wind spreads pollen. Some plants can even **self-pollinate**.

But for many flowering plants, bees are the best pollinators. Pollen must move between flowers of the same type for pollination to occur. Bees tend to visit

The hairs on a bee's body help the insect trap pollen.

one type of flower at a time. This makes pollination more likely.

Most pollinators collect pollen by accident. But bees gather pollen on purpose. As a result, they are more likely to spread it around. Fortunately, these top pollinators live all around the world. Bees live on every continent except Antarctica.

CHAPTER 2

THE BUSINESS OF BEES

More than 75 percent of the world's crops depend partly on animal pollinators. Many of these pollinators are bees. Without bees, farmers would need to find other ways to pollinate their plants. Even self-pollinating plants often produce more when pollinated by bees.

Bees pollinate many plants that produce fruit. Apple trees are one example.

Many regions don't have enough bees to handle pollination. This problem is worse in large areas where only one crop grows. In these places, plants produce flowers all at once. Many farmers must use managed honey bees for pollination.

Managed honey bees are cared for by beekeepers. Unlike most other bees, honey bees live together in colonies. Beekeepers provide hives for the colonies. The bees build honeycombs on frames inside the hives. Honeycombs are wax structures where bees store their honey.

Beekeepers make money by **renting** out their bees. When a crop is ready for pollination, beekeepers take their bees

A beekeeper pulls out a honeycomb from a managed honey bee hive.

to that area. They move the beehives in trucks. Some bee colonies are transported thousands of miles. After the crop is pollinated, the beekeepers move the hives to a new crop.

This process continues for many months. Every February, approximately 30 billion honey bees travel to California.

First, they pollinate almonds. Then the hives are moved to pollinate other crops. Honey bees pollinate apples in Washington, blueberries in Maine, and watermelons in Texas.

HONEY BEES HIT THE ROAD

Managed honey bee pollination in the United States

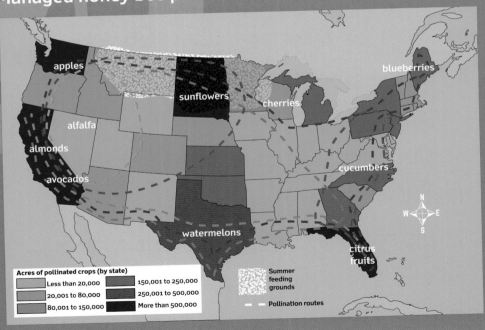

apples

sunflowers

cherries

blueberries

alfalfa

almonds

avocados

cucumbers

watermelons

citrus fruits

N
W E
S

Acres of pollinated crops (by state)

Less than 20,000	150,001 to 250,000
20,001 to 80,000	250,001 to 500,000
80,001 to 150,000	More than 500,000

Summer feeding grounds

- - Pollination routes

Managed honey bees are important pollinators. But they can threaten wild bees. "Wild bees" refers to all bees that are not honey bees. They are often **native** to an area. Managed honey bees can spread diseases to wild bees. Sometimes, they escape their hives. They compete with wild bees for non-crop food sources.

BUYING BEES BY MAIL

Honey bees are excellent pollinators. But other bee species are better at pollinating certain crops. For example, blue orchard bees are good at pollinating fruit trees. Unlike honey bees, these bees do not live together in hives. This makes them harder to manage. But many farmers still buy blue orchard bees. These bees arrive as **cocoons** in the mail.

HONEY IN HUMAN HISTORY

As pollinators, bees help produce many foods. But honey bees also make their own food. They create honey from nectar. Then they store the honey to eat in winter.

Honey bees often make more honey than they need. Beekeepers sell the extra honey. The honey's flavor depends on where it comes from. That's because different types of plants produce different flavors of nectar.

Humans have been eating honey for at least 9,000 years. Ancient cave paintings show images of humans gathering honey. Scientists have even found pots of honey in old Egyptian tombs. Tombs are large stone structures used to bury bodies. The honey from the tombs was thousands of years old. But it could still be eaten!

A beekeeper collects honey from a honeycomb.

Honey also has medical purposes. Humans have used honey as medicine for thousands of years. For example, some people put honey on cuts to prevent infection.

CHAPTER 3

BEES UNDER THREAT

Today, bees face many challenges. In 2016, seven bee species became **endangered** in the United States. In Europe, 9 percent of bees face possible **extinction**. One part of China has so few bees that people pollinate plants by hand.

Pesticides are one of the major causes of decreasing bee populations.

A woman pollinates peach blossoms by hand in Zaozhuang, China.

Some farmers use tractors to spray pesticides in large amounts.

Humans use pesticides to kill unwanted insects. But many pesticides either kill or sicken bees.

Other current farming practices also hurt bees. In the past, humans tended to have smaller farms. These farms often had a variety of crops. But today's farms tend to have large fields with only one crop. The plants in this crop bloom all at once. When the crop stops flowering, nearby bees run out of food.

The growth of cities also threatens bees. Many wild bees nest in the ground. But in cities, much of the ground is paved over. Humans replace open land with houses, shops, and other buildings. This gives bees fewer places to nest. It also leads to a decrease in wildflowers. With fewer wildflowers, bees don't have as many sources of nectar and pollen.

Several diseases and pests can harm bees. One type of mite sucks honeybees' blood. This pest can kill entire colonies.

Disease killed the honey bees on this honeycomb.

Mites spread more easily when honey bees from different places come together. This occurs when beekeepers transport bees to pollinate crops.

Climate change is another threat facing bees. This is a long-term shift in Earth's temperature and weather patterns. Rising temperatures affect when flowers bloom. Climate change also affects yearly rainfall. These changes can make it harder for bees to collect food.

THE MYSTERY OF THE VANISHING BEES

In 2006, US beekeepers made a sad discovery. Their honey bees were vanishing. Some beekeepers lost 30 to 90 percent of their colonies. They called the problem colony collapse disorder. Many beekeepers blamed pesticides. But scientists were not sure of the cause. It may have been a combination of issues, including mites, habitat changes, and disease. Fortunately, by 2014, losses from the disorder had decreased.

CHAPTER 4

SAVING THE BEES

There are many ways humans can help bees. One way is to protect bees from pesticides. Farmers can use bee-safe options for pest control. Governments can pass laws to manage pesticide use. And scientists can do more research on how to best use pesticides.

Children who want to help bees can learn from experienced beekeepers.

Farmers can also help bees by changing their farming practices. They can plant crops that bloom at different times. This will provide food for bees over longer periods. Farmers can also grow native plants between rows of crops. These plants become food sources for bees. Experts think these changes could improve crop production. Farmers and bees would both benefit.

Anyone can help bees. Not all bee **conservationists** are farmers or beekeepers. People can encourage governments to support bee research. With more support, scientists will learn more about threats to bees.

Dandelion fields help bees survive in the early spring.

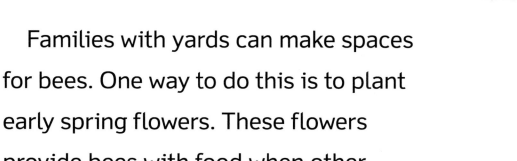

    Families with yards can make spaces for bees. One way to do this is to plant early spring flowers. These flowers provide bees with food when other sources are low. Another way is to allow dandelions to grow. These plants, often thought of as weeds, are sources of nectar and pollen.

This bee-friendly space has flowers for feeding and bare dirt for nesting.

Bees need water along with food. Families can make water gardens by filling bowls with water and rocks. The water should only partly cover the rocks. That way, bees have a place to stand while they drink.

Families can also clear a spot of bare dirt. Bees that nest in the ground can live in the cleared space. Other bees nest in wood. Families can build bee houses by drilling holes in blocks of wood.

As key pollinators, bees help a variety of plants to seed and grow. These plants provide food for people and animals. By protecting bees, people take care of many living things.

BEE-FRIENDLY CITIES

People without yards can also help bees. Some cities have community gardens. Apartment buildings can have roof gardens. Families can grow plants in these spaces to attract bees. Bees will even visit potted plants on balconies. People can also encourage cities to grow flowering plants along roadsides.

FOCUS ON
BEES

Write your answers on a separate piece of paper.

1. Write a sentence that describes the key ideas in Chapter 3.

2. Do you think farmers should stop using pesticides? Why or why not?

3. What do bees spread to help plants grow?
    - **A.** nectar
    - **B.** pesticide
    - **C.** pollen

4. How do bees help in the production of meat and dairy products?
    - **A.** They pollinate dandelions.
    - **B.** They pollinate alfalfa.
    - **C.** They pollinate almonds.

Answer key on page 32.

GLOSSARY

cocoons
Coverings that protect some insects as they grow.

conservationists
People who protect plants and animals.

endangered
In danger of dying out.

extinction
The process of an entire species dying out.

native
Living or growing naturally in a particular region.

nectar
A sweet liquid released by plants.

pollen
A fine powder produced by some plants that helps create new plants.

renting
Letting someone use something in return for payment.

self-pollinate
When a flower pollinates itself or another flower on the same plant.

species
Groups of animals or plants that are similar.

TO LEARN MORE

BOOKS

Brunelle, Lynn. *Turn This Book into a Beehive*. New York: Workman Publishing, 2018.

Chadwick, Fergus, Steve Alton, Emma Sarah Tennant, Bill Fitzmaurice, and Judy Earl. *The Bee Book*. New York: DK Publishing, 2016.

Socha, Piotr. *Bees: A Honeyed History*. New York: Abrams Books for Young Readers, 2017.

NOTE TO EDUCATORS

Visit **www.focusreaders.com** to find lesson plans, activities, links, and other resources related to this title.

INDEX

Answer Key: 1. Answers will vary; **2.** Answers will vary; **3.** C; **4.** B